Ludwig van Beethoven

MISSA SOLEMNIS
IN FULL SCORE

From the Breitkopf & Härtel
Complete Works Edition

DOVER PUBLICATIONS, INC.
NEW YORK

Published in Canada by General Publishing Company, Ltd.,
30 Lesmill Road, Don Mills, Toronto, Ontario.
Published in the United Kingdom by Constable and Company, Ltd.,
3 The Lanchesters, 162–164 Fulham Palace Road, London W6 9ER.

This Dover edition, first published in 1991,
is a republication of the edition originally published in Series 19:
Kirchenmusik from *Ludwig van Beethoven's Werke,*
Breitkopf & Härtel, Leipzig, n.d.
A translation of the texts, a glossary of German terms
and a list of instruments have been added.

Manufactured in the United States of America
Dover Publications, Inc.
31 East 2nd Street
Mineola, N.Y. 11501

Library of Congress Cataloging-in-Publication Data

Beethoven, Ludwig van, 1770–1827.
Missa solemnis : from the Breitkopf & Härtel complete works edition /
Ludwig van Beethoven.—In full score.
1 score.
For solo voices (SATB), chorus (SATB), and orchestra.
Latin words: English translation printed as text.
Reprint. Originally published: Leipzig : Breitkopf & Härtel, 1864
(Ludwig van Beethoven's Werke. Serie 19, Kirchenmusik).
ISBN 0-486-26894-2
1. Masses—Scores.   I. Title.
M2010.B43S6   1991   91-754319
                                    CIP
                                      M

Contents

Texts and Translations

Kyrie

Kyrie eleison.
Christe eleison.
Kyrie eleison.

Gloria

Gloria in excelsis Deo, et in terra pax hominibus bonae voluntatis. Laudamus te, benedicimus te, adoramus te, glorificamus te. Gratias agimus tibi propter magnam gloriam tuam. Domine Deus, Rex coelestis, Deus pater omnipotens. Domine fili unigenite, Jesu Christe, Domine Deus, agnus Dei, filius patris. Qui tollis peccata mundi, miserere nobis, qui tollis peccata mundi, suscipe deprecationem nostram, qui sedes ad dexteram patris, miserere nobis. Quoniam tu solus sanctus, tu solus dominus, tu solus altissimus, Jesu Christe, cum sancto spiritu, in gloria Dei patris, amen.

Credo

Credo in unum Deum, patrem omnipotentem, factorem coeli et terrae, visibilium omnium et invisibilium. Et in unum dominum Jesum Christum, filium Dei unigenitum, et ex patre natum ante omnia saecula. Deum de Deo, lumen de lumine, Deum verum de Deo vero, genitum, non factum, consubstantialem patri, per quem omnia facta sunt. Qui propter nos homines et propter nostram salutem descendit de coelis. Et incarnatus est de spiritu sancto ex Maria virgine; et homo factus est. Crucifixus etiam pro nobis sub Pontio Pilato, passus et sepultus est. Et resurrexit tertia die, secundum scripturas, et ascendit in coelum, sedet ad dexteram patris, et iterum venturus est cum gloria judicare vivos et mortuos, cujus regni non erit finis. Credo in spiritum sanctum, Dominum et vivificantem, qui ex patre filioque procedit, qui cum patre et filio simul adoratur et conglorificatur, qui locutus est per Prophetas. Credo in unam sanctam catholicam et apostolicam ecclesiam, confiteor unum baptisma in remissionem peccatorum, et expecto resurrectionem mortuorum, et vitam venturi saeculi, amen.

Sanctus (Benedictus)

Sanctus, sanctus, sanctus, Dominus Deus Sabaoth. Pleni sunt coeli et terra gloria tua! Osanna in excelsis. Benedictus qui venit in nomine Domini. Osanna in excelsis.

Agnus Dei

Agnus Dei qui tollis peccata mundi, miserere nobis.
Agnus Dei qui tollis peccata mundi, miserere nobis.
Agnus Dei qui tollis peccata mundi, dona nobis pacem.

Kyrie

Lord, have mercy on us.
Christ, have mercy on us.
Lord, have mercy on us.

Gloria

Glory to God in the highest, and on earth peace to men of good will. We praise thee, we bless thee, we adore thee, we glorify thee. We give thee thanks for thy great glory. Lord God, heavenly King, God the father almighty. Lord, the only-begotten son, Jesus Christ, Lord God, lamb of God, son of the father. Thou who takest away the sins of the world, have mercy on us, thou who takest away the sins of the world, receive our prayer, thou who sittest at the right hand of the father, have mercy on us. For thou alone art holy, thou alone art the lord, thou alone, Jesus Christ, with the holy ghost, art most high in the glory of God the father, amen.

Credo

I believe in one God, the father almighty, maker of heaven and earth, and of all things visible and invisible. And in one lord Jesus Christ, the only-begotten son of God, born of the father before all ages. God of God, light of light, true God of true God, begotten, not made, consubstantial with the father, by whom all things were made. Who for us men and for our salvation came down from heaven. And was incarnate by the holy ghost of the Virgin Mary; and was made man. He was crucified also for us under Pontius Pilate, suffered and was buried. And on the third day he rose again, according to the scriptures, and ascended into heaven, and sitteth at the right hand of the father, and he shall come again with glory to judge the living and the dead, and his kingdom shall have no end. I believe in the holy ghost, the Lord and giver of life, who proceedeth from the father and the son, who together with the father and the son is worshiped and glorified, who hath spoken by the Prophets. I believe in one holy catholic and apostolic church, I confess one baptism for the remission of sins, and I await the resurrection of the dead, and the life of the world to come, amen.

Sanctus (Benedictus)

Holy, holy, holy, Lord God of Hosts. Heaven and earth are full of thy glory! Hosanna in the highest. Blessed is he that cometh in the name of the Lord. Hosanna in the highest.

Agnus Dei

Lamb of God, who takest away the sins of the world, have mercy on us.
Lamb of God, who takest away the sins of the world, have mercy on us.
Lamb of God, who takest away the sins of the world, grant us peace.

Glossary of German Terms

Andacht, devotion, *mit Andacht*, devoutly
ängstlich, anxiously, timidly
äussern, outward
Bitte, prayer
einige, a few
Es, E-flat
Friede(n), peace
innern, inward
mit, with
nur, only
Preludium, prelude
um, for
und, and
Violinen, violins
zwei, two

Instrumentation

2 Flutes [Flauti]
2 Oboes [Oboi]
2 Clarinets (A, C, B♭) [Clarinetti in A, C, B]
2 Bassoons [Fagotti]
Contrabassoon [Contrafagotto]
4 Horns (D, E♭ , B♭ basso, E, G) [Corno in D, Es, B basso, E, G]
2 Trumpets (D, B♭ , C) [Trombe in D, B, C]
Alto Trombone [Trombone Alto]
Tenor Trombone [Trombone Tenore]
Bass Trombone [Trombone Basso]
Timpani
Organ [Organo]
Violins I, II [Violino]
Violas [Viola]
Cellos [Violoncello]
Basses [Basso]

Soprano
Alto   } Soloists
Tenor
Bass
Sopranos
Altos
Tenors
Basses

MISSA SOLEMNIS
in D Major
Op. 123

Dedicated to Archduke Rudolph of Austria

KYRIE

Assai sostenuto. Mit Andacht.

6

7

Andante assai ben marcato.

Tempo I.

GLORIA

cresc.
pe de-pre-ca-ti-o-nem nostram, sus - - ci-pe de-pre - - ca - - ti-o-nem no-stram,
cresc.
sus - ci-pe, sus - ci-pe de-pre-ca - ti-o-nem no-stram,
cresc.
sus - ci-pe, sus - ci-pe de-pre-ca - - ti-o - - nem no-stram,
cresc.
sus - - ci-pe de - pre-ca - - - - - - - ti-onem no-stram,
qui
qui
qui
qui
cresc.
f

58

60

Allegro maestoso.

Quo_niam tu   so _ lus sanc_tus,

Quo_ni_am tu   so_lus do__minus,

Allegro, ma non troppo e ben marcato.

68

69

74

Poco più Allegro.

glo _ _ ri _ a, glo _ ri _ a, glo _ ri _ a.
glo _ _ ri _ a, glo _ ri _ a, glo _ ri _ a.
glo _ _ ri _ a, glo _ ri _ a, glo _ ri _ a.
glo _ _ ri _ a, glo _ ri _ a, glo _ ri _ a.

CREDO

Qui pro _ pter nos ho _ mines et propter no _ _ stram sa _ lu _ tem de _ _

Qui pro _ pter nos ho _ mines et propter no _ _ stram sa _ lu _ tem

Qui pro _ pter nos ho _ mines et propter no _ _ stram sa _ lu _ tem de _ scendit de coelis,

Qui pro _ pter nos ho _ mines et propter no _ _ stram sa _ lu _ tem de _ scendit de coelis,

poco cresc.

poco cresc.

poco cresc.

poco cresc.

in F.

poco cresc.

poco cresc.

p

dim.

pp più dim.   pp

poco cresc.

dim.

pp più dim.   pp

poco cresc.

dim.

pp più dim.   pp

pas - - sus.

pas - sus.

pas - sus.

sub Ponti - o Pi - la - to pas - sus.

et   se_pul_ tus   est,_____   et se_pultus est.

et   se_pul_ tus   est,_____   et se_pultus est.

et   se_pul_ tus   est,_____   et se_pultus est.

et   se_pul _ tus   est,_____   et se_pultus   est.

p   dim.   pp

p   dim.   pp

p   dim.   pp

p   dim.   pp

poco cresc.   p   dim.   pp più dim.   pp

poco cresc.   p   dim.   pp piùdim.   pp

poco cresc.   p   dim.   pp più dim.   pp

Allegro.   Allegro molto.

glo_ri_a, cum glo_ri_a

glo_ri_a, cum glo_ri_a

glo_ri_a, cum glo_ri_a

glo_ri_a, cum glo_ri_a

ju_di_ca_re,

ju_di_ca_re,

ju_di_ca_re,

ju_di_ca_re,

Allegro con moto.

154

158

SANCTUS

Presto.

176

Sostenuto ma non troppo.

Preludium.

Andante molto cantabile e non troppo mosso.

pizz.
pizz.
qui ve-nit, qui ve-nit, be-ne-di - - - - - ctus, be-ne-
qui ve-nit, qui ve-nit, be-nedi - - - ctus qui
qui ve - - - - - - - - - - - - - nit,
in no - - - - - - mi-ne
pizz.

sis, in ex_cel _ sis, o_sanna in ex_cel _ sis! Be_ne_

sis, o_san _ na in ex_cel _ sis! Be_ne_

na, o_san_na, o_san_na, o_sanna in ex_cel _ sis! Be_ne_di _ _ _

san _ na, o_san_na, o_sanna in ex_cel _ sis!

AGNUS DEI

A _ _ _ gnus, a _ gnus De_i qui tol_lis pec_ca_ta

A _ _ _ gnus De_i qui tol_lis pec_

Allegretto vivace.
Bitte um innern und äussern Frieden.

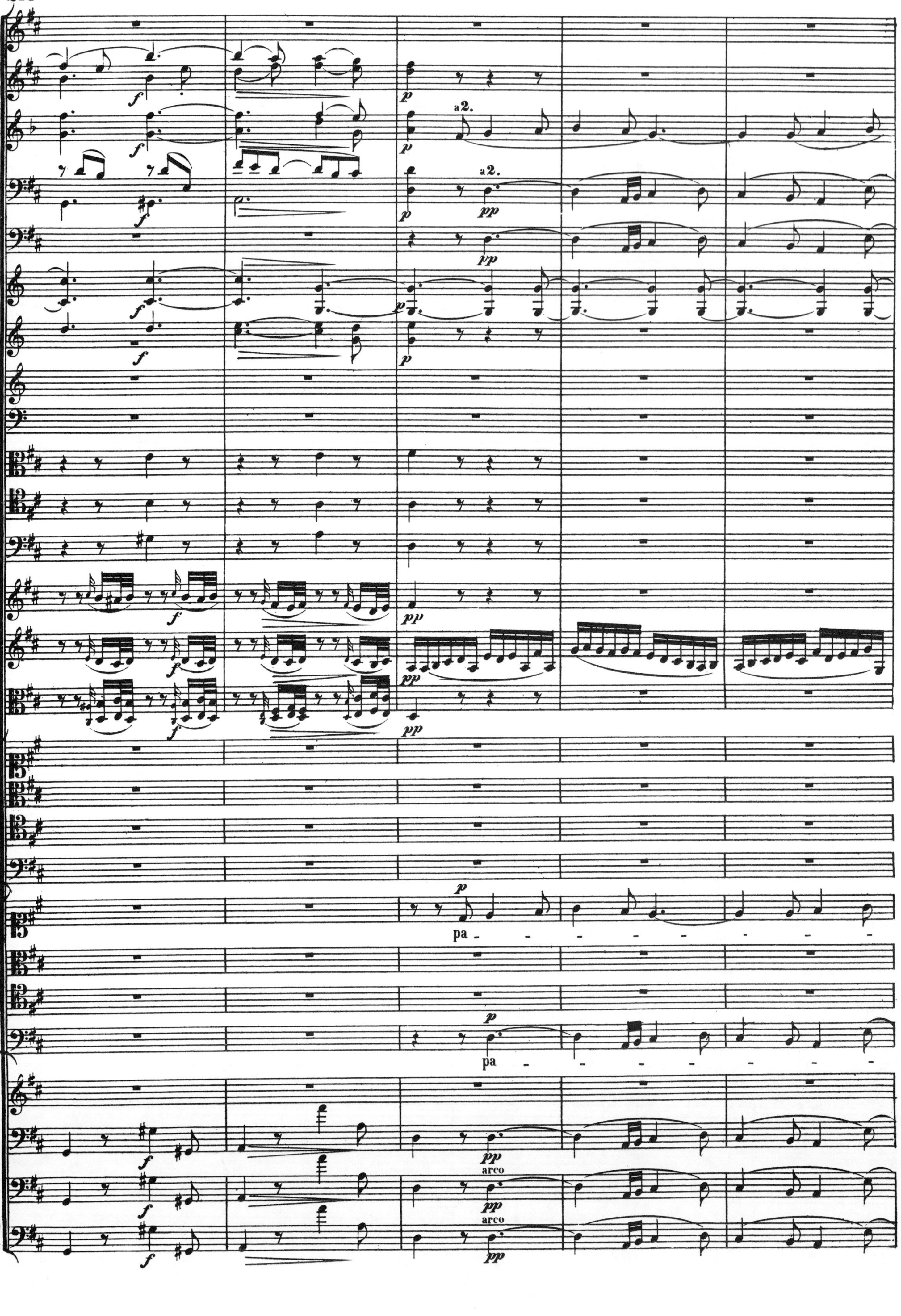
a 2.
a 2.
pa -
pa -
arco
arco

a 2.
cresc
cresc.
a 2.
cresc.
rf
a 2.
rf
rf
a 2.
rf
cresc.
rf
rf
cresc.
pa - - - cem,
cresc.
pa - -
pa - - - cem,
pa - -
pa - - - cem,

Allegro assai.

do — na

do — na

do — na

do — na

Tempo I.